Whispers from Beyond the Void

Poetry by
Carla Andrejco

Whispers from Beyond the Void
Copyright ©2021 Carla Andrejco
Cover Art Cierra Lynn Fugett 2021

ISBN- 978-1-7333822-9-8

Published by:

Blue Jade Press, LLC

Blue Jade Press, LLC
Vineland, NJ 08360
www.bluejadepress.com

Acknowledgements

To my parents for your love and support; for being proud of me even when I wasn't very proud of myself.

To my brother Nicholas, for being the most wonderful brother and friend that anyone could ask for.

To Uncle Chris, for taking me to the wonderful places that exposed me to art and culture, for indulging my curiosities and for always listening.

To my Tribe: Michelle, Alayna, Christie, Antoinette, Jenny, Bianca, Jacqui, Dominick, Josh and our dearly departed brother Jeremy. You are my spiritual family, and I love you all.

To Debra and Sarah, thank you for your friendship, sisterhood and support.

To Music House: Cierra, Brian and Mike. You are my dearest friends, and I could not do without any of you. Mike, a special thank you for helping me get my voice back.

To Anthony, for your encouragement, for all you have done for me and your part in making this possible.

To Donald "Dave" Deveney, Jr, brother, you are very much missed, very much loved and I wish you could be holding a copy of this. I hope I've done you proud.

Safe Word was previously published
New Jersey Bards Northwest Poetry Review, 2020
Local Gems Press

To Alexander, Gabriel and Elizabeth, the pearls of my world. It was always my intention that my shadows never grow so large as to be cast upon you. I dedicate this to you with all my love.

Table of Contents

Call to the Void

Light glints off of stainless-steel fear.
It catches my eye and turns my head.
You have my undivided attention.

Looking closer
I see
I stand on
blade's edge awash in cascades
of crimson rage
I drank it in as it
warmed my flesh

There is no examination
only expedition
clothing to flesh
flesh to fiber
fiber to bone
bone to blood
blood to a wet tangled jungle of viscera
beyond that
the hollow of the soul

This is where I come to rest

Eating the fruit of the vine, my mouth filled
with viscous shame that ran warm and bitter
over my tongue; I swallowed hard.

It didn't stick in the craw
but rather sank into the pit of my gut

Every particle broken down to comprehension.

I laughed in delight of it
of slitting the throats of demons
just to draw you in
I called to the void
to call you out
out of perdition and into predation
breaking chains and rattling cages
turning awkward smile to malicious grin
laughter to a growl

That call to the void, did you hear it?

Shadow

Familiar voice echoes within
day draws to close
moonlit night begins

Shadow loom and grow
creeping cold along the spine
the unknown to know

Veiled eyes
shrouded body
cloaked shoulders

Pall longings spoken only in whispers
that live through the night
and die with the dawn

Cozen

To be the lie
the plausibly denied
object clutched in child's hand
hidden behind your back

What's that you've got there?
.... nothing

Who's that you're talking to?
......................no one

Where have you been?
.................nowhere

Like the rooster that called three times
to toll the lie
thrice denied

Nothing
No one
Nowhere

Every trace
erased in an instant

Gone
Forgotten

Black Labeled

She's that stashed away bottle
don't want 'em to catch ya drinkin'
she's thinking she's
Black Labeled
necessary yet shameful

That bathtub gin behavior don't pair well with it

You talk wine cellars and overflowing casks
yet, she's a flask
tucked in the desk drawer

Just enough to get you through

The Law

I was told the law was
to Know
to Will
to Dare
to Keep Silent

All but silence I can abide

What is more feared than that which could be
spoken or heard?

The filthy hand of fear that covers the mouth
a vainglorious attempt to mute
a whimper
a scream
a chuckle
a sigh
a throaty moan

Because you cannot bear to hear
that all you dare not admit you ponder
in your quiet moments alone
I have already committed to memory

Different

My closest friends were the shadows on my wall
and the magnolia tree that bloomed every April
in the yard across the alley.
I climbed it too high once and couldn't get back
 down
So, why not just stay up there?
Up where there was nothing but the wind
clusters of Jane magnolias that gave way
to Kelly green leaves.

Solitude was a blessing, then.

Years later, I sought that tree for comfort.
One Easter morning,
I started throwing up for no reason

The prior summer found me
in a sun drenched room.
No fan to shift the breeze,
the air hung heavy and added weight
to the body above,
to the crushing fear in my chest.

I couldn't move
until a drop of sweat dripped off his face and fell
so near to my eye, it could have been a tear.

Since our sun is comprised mostly of hydrogen,
it is the perfect gas light
to accompany the gaslight
of his words.

I said, "I don't want to..."

"We're not," he said
If we were, it would sound different.

Different how?

Different like screaming STOP!?
Different like some random chick in a porno?
Different like a real apology?
Different like saying you loved me somehow
  absolves you?

Different, like what it should sound like if I said
  yes?

You mean, that kind of different?

Maybe it would have been different
if I had thought enough of myself to keep walking
past your garage when you yelled
"hey".

Maybe now I wouldn't get nauseous
every time I take my car to be serviced
or wouldn't have seen myself as enough to fuck
but not to claim.

Yeah, that kind of different.

Sacrifices

I lie prostrate
at the altar of the past
offer up my old self
to coax the phoenix
from the ash

So like me
to add fuel to the fire
but how many times
must I return to the pyre

With each return
more cinders cling
to the wings
I find flight becomes
an unbearable thing

Requiescat in Pace

There is no requiem for the death of emotion,
nothing to eulogize, no prayer for the soul
of love departed.
How can there be when
ink wells become lachrymatory bottles
for tears no one knows about?

There are no bones of memories to bury,
no regrets, no fading smiles, nothing
that could acknowledge that once
something real was there,
though there's no obituary for it.

Within myself, I had the sense of
something growing before it faded
a miscarriage of good intentions
that was too poorly formed to name,
too fragile to save.

Unknown to me, an aborted love

As I stare at an imaginary grave, I wonder
can what has never been truly be lost?
It's a trick of the mind; a corpse
I can still see
breathing
hoping
beyond hope
it is peacefully at rest and will rise again.

One by one,
I drive nails into the lid of a box
where something should lie in repose.
My hands begin trembling.
I cannot drive the last nail.
What lies there is a part of my very
 self.
How could I bear to be buried alive?

Safe Word

Love hurts in its truest forms
of stocking and jumper covered bruises
split lips and dissociative responses.
Love wore rage home from the bars,
caused invisible scars and converted me

You see,
Safe, for me, may as well be Antarctica.

A place which I know
but wouldn't ever plan to go.
My grandfather sailed
there when he was in the Navy.
once upon a time.
It's a truth that can be acknowledged
but not a truth that's mine.

I know gaslight, devaluation and discard.
Make up hides the hours of skin picking,
but you can't see my scars.

I know arctic apologies, remote and cold, yet
native.

Love your enemy and pray for those
who hate you.
And in Jesus' name she prayed,
"Take my hands should I ever strike her again"
But mother, you prayed the wrong prayer.

You never prayed "deliver her from chiding
envy and false charm".
You prayed to stop hitting
but not to stop doing harm.

Love hurts,
and that's all I know.

Maybe I'll see love one day as some exotic locale
the Caymans, the Carpathians

Warm desert painted skies open
no need to hide, when
"I'm ok" stops being a story everyone's heard
then maybe "safe" will be my safe word

Boy

Boy stepped out onto his porch
boy's sister slipped past him
met me at the sidewalk
hissing through a smile

"I hate that bitch"
boy stood silent

Boy's eyes met mine when
boy's new girlfriend appeared
boy looked at me in horror when
she slipped her hand in his

Boy looked confused when I
laughed and shook my head
while boy's sister
spoke to my friend

Boy already knew that
I wasn't proud of what I'd do
but you brought this on yourself,
Boy

Boy didn't hear when boy's sister
asked me "you gonna fuck her up?"
and I said yeah, but
I don't have to touch her

Boy fucked me up
didn't lay a hand on me
I just learned the truth
and I guess we're even now

Contact

A day goes dark and is rendered mute.
It's a night for TV noise
simply for the sake
of remembering a human voice.
to cry at comedy
because I'm either not in on the joke or I'm the
butt of it

Cry out the ghost of the God of my childhood
"I really fucking need you right now"
there is only silence
and anyone I would speak to
would ask the dreaded question
"are you okay?"

I can hear the repetitious chant of the voice in
their heads they think no one else can hear
"please say you're ok"
"please say you're ok"
"please say you're ok"

You're off the hook

Even if I could say that I'm not
to go there would be like asking someone
drowning to take a deep breath

There's already enough water
in my lungs
in my eyes
in my soul
the murky fluid of a little girl's sad voice
man's indifference
a stark reminder that my mother named me
"strength"
to get me through nights like these

Through nights though already bloodied and
beaten, I have to keep shadow boxing
every blow must be landed, every swing must
make contact

Every punch fueled by anger, because when I
cried out to God that I am in desperate need of
contact

This is NOT what I meant

i ~~hate~~ you

everything was fine
I would wake up in the morning
live every day in quietude
I had my routine, my certainty
and it was okay

and then we shook hands
and I shook your hand like
the girl in the library
who really wanted to be left alone
but motioned to the empty chair next to her
shook your hand
like there was space at the table
like who put that chair there?

like "who invited this guy?"

and then my phone rang every morning
or I'd get a text and
you freaked out a bit when I answered slow
like
who does that?

I mean, I do that but that's not the point

The point is

why the fuck are you doing that?

Then we meet for coffee and
you have the gall to ask ME
"will I see you again?"
because
a very real part of me wanted to slap
the affection right out of your mouth

Wanted you to start to choke on the words
like a sip of something hot that went down
the wrong way

Because maybe this went down the wrong way

With that wide eyed, back hand at the ready
like momma pissed on a Sunday
"don't you make me..." trails off to a
gritted teeth murmur

And when I drove two hours to see you
in the rain you called while I was
on the way to check
if I'm okay

Who the hell do you think you are?

At first sign of trouble
you apologize first
you own your part before I can
even try to apologize for
making you apologize

What is wrong with you?

And when I needed to take a step back
your sobs trailed behind me like
a chill in the air I couldn't shake
like
I mattered
or some bullshit like that

Don't do that

Don't call me at 3am
just because I'm upset
don't remind me how you
disturb my peace

Remind me that my peace
is isolation
is self-reliance in the extreme
is fear of vulnerability
is me with a sword at the ready
is me armored
is me in the dark room
in a tower I built too high
and you weren't foolish enough
to try and scale it
no

you stayed down there and
dodged arrows
chipped away at the mortar

Until the cracks started to show

Until it fell apart

You looked up and me
all smug like
now what?

Proud of yourself for fucking it up
taking out a wall to
make the window to my world bigger

YOU RUINED EVERYTHING

thank you

Remain to Pray

I thought that though you'd come to scoff
you might remain to pray
most aren't looking for who owes them
they're looking for who will pay

But I've paid my dues and settled my scores
as comfortable in a halo as I am in horns

Some are more at ease with fear and denial
that's the price for mixing the cause and cure
in the same vial

Drink the poison and wait for them to die
I keep my concoctions separate
I have nothing to hide

I can accept another's darkness, but they are ill-
prepared for mine

It is in between worlds that I dwell
beset by dichotomy
a heaven and hell reign equally within me

In a world that can only choose between
vestal virgin and whore
duality is incomprehensible
often feared and seldom adored

In the garden of my soul
Lilith met Eve and entwined
ask and the gates will open
seek and you will find

somewhere where light meets shadow the divide
between night and day
who will be the one who came to scoff, but
remain to pray?

Firing Line

The curse I cannot seem to break
a target on my back that's full of holes.
I hear the gun go off
and I wonder whether the bullet
will stray this time.
I cannot seem to step out of the firing line.

Another cute brunette thing to add the sting
to put salt in the wound.
Another story to justify what I already know
is a lie, another tale to spin?
I'm bleeding through the bandage again.

Another's Tears

One day, the phone rang
phones hung on walls then
coiled cable stretched nearly
scraping the floor, coiled cable
leaves depressions in the wrist
if wrapped too tightly

I won't tell you how I know that

Sophomore English teacher calls,
calls me by my mother's name

I could have gotten away with it
more often than not the voice on the
other end returns my hello
with a puzzled utterance of her name

I had inherited my mother's voice

My mother's voice screamed
"You little bitch!"
before her hands became a
hive of agitated hornets
swarming

Screamed through my mouth
when my boy wouldn't get to bed
fast enough to hide the shakes

Her sobs ricochet off the walls
of the echo chamber of my lap,
Knees meet forehead
I remember the night she cradled me
and sobbed into my hair.

Never did I think I would hear it again

Until one September night
before the earth beneath me shook
as I screamed into the void
"GOD, THIS FUCKING HURTS!"

Yet in a second encore
on a cold grey Sunday afternoon
her sobs slid down the sleeve
of my pull over and fell onto
the pavement

"I love you, Kit Kat, and I'm so sorry for what I
put you through"

I'm sorry, I'm so sorry
I'm sorry, I'm so sorry

Steady

This is where the road bends without signage
there is no such thing as "lost" on this journey
courage, now
trembling hands
cannot still
trembling hands
gently
now
close your eyes
breathe in
let it out
love, first
kindness, first
ever and always in all things, remember this
when taken aback
know that forward is still the way
Steady, now
Steady

Tether

Open another wound
close another day
feel a little more of me
start to slip away

Tether me again?

Reel me in when
my soul unravels
give me rest when
my mind travels

To places where brave men dare not go

Tether me again

The Voice

On a stormy morning
I rise too soon
trying to decode messages from the moon
song on the radio plays
I know there's something amiss
don't betray me with a Judas kiss
paid in the silver pieces of all that could be
I have a healthy respect for well-earned scars
and revelations while driving in the car
a voice in a dream says that neither and both of us
are deceived
While the world turns at imperceptible speed,
I ask for courage to not see yet believe

Depth Perception

Still waters run deep, or so I've been told
and the stillness leads me to believe
that beneath the ripples of the fabric of
his shirt, there was depth.

So I dove in

The warning sign on every swimming pool of my
  childhood made sense.

I had then become the stick figure hitting bottom,
bolts of lightning shooting from my neck
I was made a caricature
the warning label others giggle at
that's understandable

I laughed too
and so did he

Complication

Sleep doesn't come easily these days so
I think a little
drink a little
when the music dies
cry a little.

It's not something from which you can simply
  remove yourself
not a situation from which you politely excuse
  yourself
so you find ways to amuse yourself

Until your heart starts working on your head
  again

Everyone has their advice
"what will be will be"
"cut your losses, time will heal"
I have my own opinions, but these pearls of
wisdom aren't going to change the way I feel.

It doesn't change the fact that
I still smell you in my clothes
that your shadow over my shoulder is the most
beautiful thing I ever did see
that anywhere you are
is where I'd rather be

You see, my greatest hopes
are still fighting with my greatest fears
I can still hear your voice ringing in my ears
your kiss was sweeter still

I take my heart from off my sleeve
place it in your hands
do what you will

Since sleep won't come easily today so
I think a little
drink a little
when the music dies
I'll cry a little

Curio

No wonder they call her "Curio"
an unusual rare object
a collector's piece indeed
as long as she doesn't speak
doesn't feel
doesn't need

To some one of a collection
to others one of a kind

Ever and always to a shelf consigned

Delivered into hands either
too cautious or too clumsy

Some strange in-between
never left the box and
damaged in transport
she is souled "as is"
as is, never enough
or far too much
for a Curio

Black Wing

Caw me "good morning"
perched on the tree outside,
ever reminding me that All Father
gave an eye for wisdom

Seems a small price

Since the creator in His infinite wisdom gives us
two eyes to see
two ears to hear
two hands to work;
the heir and the spare

Yet only one mind to think
one heart to feel
one mouth to speak
a wealth of words bottle necked at the throat –
the intersection between knowing and feeling

Daily, Black Wing you remind me
all I need to know, I've known
all I need to feel, I'd felt
All I need to say, I'll say

You caw me "good morning", then fly away

A Day, A Head Of
(for Nicole)

Alarm sounds and I was dreaming, distracted by
wakefulness, I forget sleeping's beauty

Fucking reality, always messing things up

See, they slap a warning label on everything
  nowadays
except on life

Woman: contents under pressure
Man: Object in mirror may appear
  closer than it is
Child: Handle with care
Heart: Contents easily broken
Mind: Contents Unstable

All of this within moments of waking

The window tells me it's snowing
I think of a friend and tell them that I love them
and hate them in equal and unbiased proportion
by way of a series of carefully selected memes

I doubt this is what David Bowie meant when he
penned "Modern Love," but I do my best.

Pride: Harmful if NOT swallowed

Despite the weather,
The day begrudgingly cooperates
I drop the kids off and beseech the universe:
"Show me the next right thing"
If I'm not paying attention when you do
and if I blow it all to hell
which I will

Keep me humble enough to own it and make
  amends

With a tank full of gas and a heart full of
  gratitude,
I head to work, but first, coffee

Coffee: Contents Hot
Work: May Cause Drowsiness

I drive by the river
because it's twenty minutes of peace
even with the blaring volume of the radio
songs that constantly remind me that
there is no decibel louder
than the rhythm of a wounded heart.

Bitch, change the station!

Too late, I've already arrived at work
I am the consummate masochist

Boss: Approach with caution

As the day goes on I'm surprised
at how productive I've been
even though I have 2 college degrees
I cannot figure out how to leave a group text

Smart Phone: Warning, Highly Corrosive

It's already dark when I get back to my car
I'm smiling because my music app suggested a
  song I might like

It's painfully exquisite
and some asshole just quoted the lyrics
in a status update

Damnit, can I keep nothing to myself?!

Temperament: Store in a cool dry place

Get home, make dinner, check in with the
parents, everyone is healthy and happy

Family: Store in a secure place

Chores, bedtime stories and tuck-ins before
scrolling and hitting "Like" a bunch of times,
maybe throw in a "Share" for good measure

Social Media: Avoid contact with eyes

Yeah, not happening

Crawl into bed where I can shamelessly spoon
with my inner thoughts, ask my heart and my
brain to be quiet for five damn minutes, though
they never listen

I love to speak to deaf ears

Feelings: Read all instructions carefully

But they're printed in five different languages and
while I was flipping through trying to find
instructions in English, something broke and it
appears there's a piece missing

Relationships: Some assembly required
Love: No refunds or exchanges

So, how do I put this together?
Oh, look, the English page!

I am constantly featured on the gag reel

With my eyes finally heavy enough for sleep, I
take a moment before I drift off to find five things
to be grateful for:

Kids are happy
House is warm
A nice compliment from a friend
Tomorrow is pay day
I survived my own brain

Sleep: Apply as often as necessary

Keening

Grief is hard enough at a death
but to mourn the living is
a hell unto itself

there is life
there is breath

a smile
a heartbeat

Conversations turn to dirges
and the worst of it
is the realization that
it was not they that passed, but I

a mourner at my own funeral

A Cry Only Heaven Can Hear

The only living, breathing thing in the room is me
my head slumped, shoulders heaving
the fissure in my heart widened to a chasm

All I feel erupts
layers of love and loss made molten burn
within my chest

A sound escapes, and in that moment
I do not call out to God,
I only hope there is one

Because it is a cry only heaven can hear
and a loneliness only the damned can know

Apostate

Like Templars or Conquistadors
they came to conquer
In the name of God, or of power
or to lay their own blame

This native is not restless
she is in repose
for her ways are ancient

They lived and breathed
when the Sacred Fire of Vesta
still burned bright
until Theodosius thought to snuff it out

How much darker and colder it became
an ideal breeding ground for growing shame

Still, the fires burned
for Druid
for Shaman
for Houngan and Mambo
for Vedma
for Medicine Man

Still, they came from the churches,
and the temples
the whore houses
and the taverns

From the sides of women clutching their pearls
and the vicars that cried "heresy"
only to find that the fires were still burning

What you call taboos, they venerate
What you call sinful, they call sacred

Go back to your priests
and your preachers
back to your wine and your women

Tell them you could not put the fires out
That they'd rather bleed from the throat than
 recant
or burn than repent

The Mirror

Fogged over and without reflection, a swipe of
my hand gives me a moment's clarity
before the edges bleed and I am blinded again

I seek not to validate, nor to compliment bait,
but to understand.
What is it that I do not see?

I have tried to divide myself, to be on both sides
of a two-way mirror.

This exercise in futility brings me no comfort, no
truth, no way to break the curse of the insatiable
desire for comprehension.

No end to the quest for the holy grail, the golden
chalice from which I may imbibe the answer to
the every "why?"

No knights required, only one to hold the mirror
and reflect me back to myself.

Touchstones

The smell of petrichor and flowers in bloom
The voices of my children

The French press on the counter in a friend's
kitchen and the embrace of those
always happy to see me

A pocket in the universe where hours are spent
speaking on existentialism, music and the moon

How my brother can make me double over with
  laughter

My parent's pride, even when I didn't deserve it

Weighted piano keys

The scent of fresh coffee and the pages of old
  volumes

Honeysuckle on the wind of a June evening

The shade of the trees along the riverbank

How the full moon always moves past my
  window

Rumbles of thunder on a stormy Saturday
  morning

The first sight of changing leaves like licks of
  flame in the trees

A lazy afternoon with Gershwin and a good book

When the winds turn cold and my nemeses are
breathing down my neck
these are the mainstays
the benchmarks
the touchstones

Gathering Shells

Bare soles meet warm sand
the taste of salt on my lips
cool water laps at my ankles
I, pointing to the horizon line
"Mommy, I want to swim out there"

Past the delicate thunder of the breakers where
everything is diamonds and aquamarine

I gathered buckets of shells;
some to keep
some to give
some to adorn the castles
where I dreamed to live someday

Ever so grand
the castles I built of pure white sand
until the tides washed them away

But it was no matter
a new castle was built again the next day

Complete with moat, flags of seaweed and
  driftwood drawbridges

Then, the castle became a fortress…
no driftwood for a drawbridge
no tide to wash it away
nowhere on the shore left for my little girl to play

I brought that little girl back to the water's edge
filled the moat
called in the tide
wiped the tears from her eyes

We watched the fortress wash out to the sea

With her pail and shovel
on her knees in the sand she fell

Build your castle, little girl
while I gather shells

Carla Andrejco was born in Trenton, NJ and lived in the Mercer County area until she moved to Alexandria, VA in 2008 where she grew up.

She returned to New Jersey in 2013 and lives in Hunterdon County. Her work has been featured in the International Library of Poetry's Perceptions of Infinity and The New Jersey Bards Northwest Poetry Review.

She is the proud mother of three children and in addition to writing enjoys music, film and visiting river towns.

"Whispers from Beyond the Void" is a journey through trauma and addiction recovery, and how seeing "through a mirror darkly" colors life experience. As the glass becomes clearer, there are painful revelations, but most importantly, hope.